TRU AUTUMN BELL

Southwest Florida Travel Guide

Discovering the Hidden Gems for Non-Beach Days

Copyright © 2024 by Tru Autumn Bell

All rights reserved. No part of this publication may be reproduced, stored or transmitted in any form or by any means, electronic, mechanical, photocopying, recording, scanning, or otherwise without written permission from the publisher. It is illegal to copy this book, post it to a website, or distribute it by any other means without permission.

Tru Autumn Bell asserts the moral right to be identified as the author of this work.

Tru Autumn Bell has no responsibility for the persistence or accuracy of URLs for external or third-party Internet Websites referred to in this publication and does not guarantee that any content on such Websites is, or will remain, accurate or appropriate.

Designations used by companies to distinguish their products are often claimed as trademarks. All brand names and product names used in this book and on its cover are trade names, service marks, trademarks and registered trademarks of their respective owners. The publishers and the book are not associated with any product or vendor mentioned in this book. None of the companies referenced within the book have endorsed the book.

First edition

This book was professionally typeset on Reedsy. Find out more at reedsy.com

Contents

1 Introduction   1
2 Naples   4
3 Bonita Springs   14
4 Fort Myers   23
5 Sanibel & Captiva Islands   34
6 Marco Island   42
7 Conclusion   47
8 Journal   49
9 Resources   52

1

Introduction

Welcome to "Southwest Florida Guide: Discovering the Hidden Gems for the Non-Beach Days." I'm thrilled you have chosen my pocket guide of the region I hold dear—Southwest Florida. First and foremost, you should know I'm a huge beach nut and I love wildlife. When it's sunny, you'll find me either at the beach or hanging with animals I love. However, I am fully aware that some are not fond of the beach or prefer alternatives for those rainy days, sunburned-looking like a lobster days to just wanting a cost-effective day trip.

This book does not by any means infer that I have included every possible adventure one could embark upon while journeying through Southwest Florida on vacation, business or relocating to the great state. After all this is a pocket book travel guide not an in-depth encyclopedia and aren't you glad for that?

Through the years of owning a car service in Naples, Florida, I often heard the $5 million dollar question at some point of the drive, "what's to do in Naples when it rains?" or "any fun things I can do with my family that won't break the bank?" Even my neighbor, Lawrence, asked me what to do in Naples; my girlfriend is coming and she's not a beach fan?" Frankly, the best way for an absolute, amazing adventure is just to get in the car and drive. Stay off of Interstate 75, venture beyond the usual tourist spots taking nothing but back roads and you'll soon discover the small, charming towns along the way and the breathtaking views of what makes Florida, well, Florida. But, if you're not into this type of adventure, no worries, I have you covered.

This pocket guide is thoughtfully divided into five sections, each dedicated to a different city, beginning with Naples, the city I proudly call home. It encompasses Naples, Bonita Springs, Ft. Myers, Marco Island, and the Sanibel/Captiva Islands. Each gem I have chosen from the cities above can take up to an hour to two hours to get there from that particular city. Before I forget to mention, we do have two seasons in Southwest Florida: In Season and Off Season. No joke. In Season refers to the end of November through April when the seasonal residents, tourists and vacationers come and 'take-over'. Off Season refers to May through October when most of the seasonal residents and tourists have headed back to their official homes and it's also our rainy and hurricane season beginning in June and lasts till September.

Knowing our two seasons is actually super relevant when it comes to drive time, crowds, and costs. I personally love our Summers: the sunsets are especially colorfully spectacular each evening, crowds are nil and bargains are plentiful for restaurants, hotels, airbnb's, etc. I know it's a bit hot in our summers but we now have a/c so you won't melt. I suggest experiencing Southwest in off- season but to each its own. Either way the hidden gems of each of these cities are filled with fun-filled lasting memories.

You should know I won't be listing the best beaches or yet one more amusement park in this guide. On a rainy day, who wants to go to the beach or to an amusement park? Plus, everyone knows Naples has the best beaches. There I said it. Let's move on.

2

Naples

Naples is my home and I really love my town. If you decide to visit Naples or relocate to Naples, you'll soon discover how beautiful Naples is with pristine beaches, lush reserves, prehistoric looking birds, luxurious shopping and fine dining.

Fun Fact: Charles Lindbergh used to fly his plane into Naples to gather supplies and such and then zip on over to Fort Myers to visit his friend, Thomas Edison.

Restaurants:

If you enjoy casual dining without paying five star prices, check these eateries while you're on your hidden gem quest:

- **Harold's Place**: 2555 Tamiami Trail North, Naples, FL34103 [Tiki Bar by the pool atmosphere; known for their hamburgers, etc. **Most visitors have no idea Harold's Place exist** Shhh, don't tell.]
- **LowBrow Pizza and Beer**: 3148 Tamiami Trail E., Naples,

FL 34112 [An eclectic hangout with out of this world, chicken wings and garlic knots.]
- **Blueberry's**: 3350 Tamiami Trail North, Naples, FL 34103 [Best breakfast hands down; my favorite dish is their Eggs Benedict.]
- **Joe's Diner**: 9331 Tamiami Trail North, Naples, FL 34108 [50's vibe and great food with generous portions.]
- **Seed to Table:** 4835 Immokalee Rd, Naples, FL 34110 [Alfie Oakes is the owner and contributes to the community big time. This place has several restaurants inside along with grocery items, a beer bar, a wine bar, a bakery, an icecream bar, coffee bar, and a freshly made pasta bar. To me it is the DisneyLand for adults and their smash burgers rock.]

Hidden Gems:

Shy Wolf Sanctuary
1161 27th St SW
Naples, FL 34117
Shywolfsanctuary.org
Note: By reservation only

Shy Wolf Sanctuary homes over 60 exotic animals who have been rescued and are unreleasable. This place gives you a tour of these animals and educates the public on how to coexist with wildlife. My clients who have taken my advice on this hidden gem are never disappointed. In fact, they were so excited they couldn't stop talking about all the wolves, cougars, foxes, and other animals they saw and what they learned. Believe me, this gem will not disappoint. Incidentally, the sanctuary offers opportunities to partner with their amazing rescue operation through many of their fundraising events and educational programs.

Gordon River Greenway
1596 Goodlette-Frank Road
Naples, FL 34105
GordonRiverGreenway.org
Cost: None

The Gordon River Greenway of 140 acres is tucked away in urban Naples yet most visitors have no idea it exists in plain sight. This is one of my absolute favorite places to hike, view the 'prehistoric' birds and the gators (word to the wise: adhere to the signage of staying on the boardwalk and never feed the gators or the birds). Make a day of it and pack a picnic. You'll want to stay for hours guaranteed. The Greenway is family friendly and dog friendly; there's even a dog park on site divided by the big dog area and the small dog area. You see they thought of everything when designing this gem in the heart of Naples.

Here are a few of amenities of the Gordon River Greenway that I appreciate immensely and I surmise you will too:

- Wildlife viewing stations
- Picnic shelters
- Paved pathways and decorative bridges
- Restrooms (Yay!)
- Playground
- Canoe/Kayak launch

Holocaust Museum & Cohen Education Center
975 Imperial Golf Course Blvd
Naples, FL 34110
Hmcec.org
Cost: $8-$15

The Holocaust Museum & Cohen Education Center stands as a poignant testament to the preservation of Holocaust memories and history, while simultaneously emphasizing the critical importance of Holocaust education and human rights awareness. Offering both guided and self-guided audio tours, the museum provides a deeply informative and reflective experience for its visitors.

I deeply value the comprehensive approach they take in educating the public, particularly through their GenShoah programs which include films, speakers, and plays. This method of engagement is not only incredibly informative but also essential in today's society.

Some other memorable nuggets the Holocaust museum offers are over 1,000 artifacts and photographs. The museum even houses a 10-ton Holocaust railway boxcar used in the German railway during WWII. This boxcar earned recognition as the only traveling boxcar exhibit. It doesn't travel anymore since it's now over a hundred years old but such a memorable artifact.

May we never forget what happened to the Jews during this horrific time in history or we will be doomed to repeat it. It is good for our souls that we honor the precious lives lost and applaud those who fought fiercely to survive, share their story and be heard by all humanity.

Take the time to visit this museum while you're here in Naples. You'll be glad you did.

CREW Bird Rookery Swamp
　1295 Shady Hollow Blvd W
　Naples, FL 34120
　Crewtrust.org
　Cost: None

If you're into hiking, biking, bird watching, walking and/or horseback riding, you're gonna love the CREW Bird Rookery Swamp. Twelve miles of trails to your heart's content filled with an array of spectacular birds such as spoon bills, barred owls, painted buntings, cranes, and blue herons. Then, of course, the other wildlife that lives within the twelve miles that will certainly take your breath away such as panthers, alligators, otters, bobcats, deer, and yes, snakes. I'm personally not a fan of snakes, but I know they are absolutely necessary for the ecosystem. Don't judge me.

Here's the thing that you need to really embrace when embarking on these trails. Many of the trails are on dirt paths that can get rather muddy during the rainy season so dress appropriately. Make sure your shoes are closed-toe too. There is a 1500 ft boardwalk which is super helpful and by the way wheelchair accessible, but the wildlife didn't get the memo that the boardwalk is for humans. You may encounter wildlife on the boardwalk. Keep your distance and give the wildlife their space. It is after all their habitat and they are allowing us to be there. I'm assuming they are allowing our presence.

The CREW offers maps for the trails as well as useful suggestions when hitting the trails. Do take heed to their advice. I've not personally seen a panther on the trails but I know others who have. Great photography right? But avoid taking the selfie with them; panthers, poisonous snakes and alligators don't appreciate selfies at all.

I would also suggest checking out their website before going because they keep it updated frequently with information regarding the condition of the trails that may be too wet to blaze or if they are working on a certain section to restore and replenish.

Here are the names of the trails at the CREW:

- CREW Marsh Trails: Best time to see our colorful Florida flowers is in the Summer.
- CREW Cypress Dome Trails: Also known as The Wild

Coffee Trail; this trail offers hunting, of course, during hunting season with a hunting permit.
- CREW Flint Pen Strand Trails: Also known as the Purple Trail with hunting allowed. Check the hunting dates. No hunting is allowed anywhere near the hiking trails.This trail is approximately 3.1 miles to the Bird Rookery Swamp and 3.1 miles back.

As for horseback riding, you will need a permit to do this (located on their website for you to download). The CREW does not provide the horses; you need to bring your own and I believe you're allowed up to 4 or 5 horses. I have a few clients who live seasonally in Naples but have transported their favorite horses to board here and enjoy taking their horses to hit the trails. Something definitely to consider.

These trails, while challenging for the faint of heart, are immensely rewarding and worth your time and effort. They offer the opportunity to create beautiful memories and immerse yourself in nature, providing a much-needed sense of calm for the soul.

Bottom-line is always be aware of your surroundings. Be alert and heed any signage warnings. You'll be fine and you'll have bragging rights too.

This section of the travel guide has aimed to not only navigate you through these hidden marvels but also to connect you deeply with the soul of Naples, ensuring that your journey here becomes a collection of unforgettable moments. Whether you're a seasoned traveler, a seasonal resident or a curious local, Naples, with its understated charm and hidden corners, is a destination that promises to enchant and surprise.

3

Bonita Springs

Bonita Springs, strategically situated between Naples and Ft. Myers is fondly known as the Gateway to the Gulf. Just a mere 15-minute journey from Naples, this charming town holds a special place in my heart, having been my home during my college years. Even now, I find myself frequently drawn back to Bonita Springs, not only for its nostalgic value but also for the myriad of hidden gems it continues to offer.

Fun Fact: Bonita Springs was initially called Survey, the city underwent a renaming to Bonita Springs in the early 20th century. It was renamed to better appeal to those moving to the city because of the booming citrus grove industry.

Restaurants:

I prefer dining on a dime so I chose a few locations that are my favorite to frequent.

- **Grandpa's Pizza**: 27030 Old 41 Road, Bonita Springs, FL 34135 [My family and I have been eating Grandpa's pizza for over thirty years. Point of agitation: Grandpa seriously has not aged even a little since my college days. Yes, he's still in the kitchen making the best Italian pies. Our favorite pie is Grandpa's Special. Have Grandpa drizzle garlic oil on the pizza too. Oh, my goodness, I'm craving pizza now.]

- **Doc's Beach House**: 27908 Hickory Blvd, Bonita Springs, FL 34134 [Doc's has been around forever too. All the locals love Doc's Beach House. The food is delicious and casual. We're so proud of Doc's getting their restaurant backup and running again after Hurricane Ian blasted through.]

- **Doug's Seafood**: 3411 Bonita Beach Road, unit 307, Bonita Springs, FL 34134 [Best friend seafood in town. Lobster bisque is to die for and reasonably priced. Oh, and get the shoestring onion rings too.]

- **Buffalo Chips**: 26620 Old 41 Road, Bonita Springs, FL 34135 [Another staple of Bonita Springs and has been around for forty years. Chicken wings, BBQ, fried green tomatoes and fried mushrooms are just a few of my favorites at this legendary restaurant that we, locals, adore.]

- **Downtown Coffee and Wine Company:** 27546 Old 41 Road, Bonita Springs, FL 34135 [I enjoy a good coffee shop where the coffee is roasted and ground locally and the ambiance is peaceful. You will find your perfect brew or wine here. It is so relaxing to sit outside under the white decorative lights and curl up on a loveseat, read my book and sip my coffee.]

- **Trackside Donuts**: 28001 Old 41 Road, Bonita Springs, FL 34135 [These donuts are the bomb, bigger and better is their mantra and they aren't playing. It's located in a tiny A-frame building on the corner of Old 41 and Bonita Beach Road. They have limited hours because they sell out so fast. Officially, they close the doors at 1p every day but if they sell out sooner, the doors get closed sooner. That's how good the donuts are.]

Hidden Gems:
  Wonder Gardens
  27180 Old 41 Road,
  Bonita Springs, FL 34135
  Wondergardens.org
  Cost: $8-$12

The Wonder Gardens also known as The Everglade Wonder Gardens has been around since 1936. As a kid I loved coming here and as an adult I still do. This place rescues, rehabilitates and houses those who are unreleasable from Florida's flamingos, alligators, macaws, turtles, pythons to Chinese Golden Pheasants. Plus, they also have beautiful botanical gardens. Definite opportunities for photos. Hint-Hint.

I've also heard of some couples getting married here. Maybe you and your honey will be next.

Riverside Park
  10450 Reynolds St.
  Bonita Springs, FL 34135
  CityofBonitaSprings.org
  Cost: None

Riverside Park is smack dab in the middle of downtown Bonita Springs. The park often features outdoor movies in the Summer; you just have to bring your own chair and snacks. The movies are free and family friendly.

Every holiday they decorate the park according to the theme of the holiday but Christmas is my favorite. They go all out on decorations. But, they also host art festivals, church services, and concerts.

Riverside Park features the Bandshell, Butterfly Garden, Artist Cottages, Liles Hotel, 9/11 Memorial and the Fountain. Stop at the local ice-cream shop across the street and enjoy a leisure walk around the park or rent a bike from the bike shop, Engels Bicycle shop, which is right around the corner from the park. But, my favorite feature of Riverside is the canoe/kayak launching dock. You can rent a kayak there at the park or bring your own. Kayaking on the Imperial River will certainly make your day as you slowly meander through the crooks and bends of the river. You'll find this park very cozy and inviting for the perfect afternoon.

Koreshan's State Park
　3800 Corkscrew Road
　Estero, FL 33928
　FriendsofKoreshan.org
　Cost: $5.00

I know; I know this park has an Estero address but it's so close to Bonita Springs. You can literally drive on Tamiami Trail through Bonita Springs and go another 7 miles and it's right there on your right.

I have fond memories of this historical site and spending the day with just my dad as we walked the grounds of the 1894 pioneers.

Buildings are still erect and you can get tours of this landmark. The Koreshans were a religious sect with some unusual views and when their leader died in 1908, their vision died with him.

About 200 people joined the Koreshans movement during the 1900's but eventually in 1961, the remaining Koreshans donated the 305 acres to Florida as a historical landmark. The remaining five members of the 200 were allowed to live on the settlement till their deaths and the last one passed away in 1982.

You can visit the Koreshan Park and learn more about their way of life through guided tours and how they survived in this patch of land back in the early 1900's. Not an easy task by any means because Florida in the 1900's was swamp land and the terrain was unforgiving. The park offers blacksmith demonstrations, historic cooking programs, and the antique engines of the Koreshan machine shops. Farmer's Market is on Sundays but always check their website for their next event where they feature concerts and ghost walks.

Cullum's Bonita Trail
27601 Kent Road
Bonita Springs, FL 34135
Cost: None

One of the best kept secrets of Bonita Springs is the Cullum's Bonita Trail. It's a mostly shaded loop trail that is quite peaceful, remote and tranquil with some great river views too as the trail goes along the Imperial River.

Note: There is a restroom facility at the beginning of the trail and the only restroom on the trail.

The banyan trees throughout the trail makes your walk even more scenic. There's even an exercise station along the way with rough looking exercise equipment. I guess this is for those over achievers.

I will add that I wouldn't call this a wheelchair accessible type of trail. Most of the trail is dirt and it could be quite difficult to navigate a wheelchair.

This ends the section of Bonita Springs' trove of hidden gems waiting for you to discover. These treasures are both enchanting and memorable for those of you seeking the less-traveled path.

4

Fort Myers

Fort Myers is as far North as we will journey in this pocket travel guide. It's about a 45 minute drive from Naples with some definite fun things to do. The city is much larger than Naples and Bonita Springs and as you may have guessed, has great beaches. However, hurricane Ian did significant damage to the Fort Myers Beach in 2022 and is in recovery mode. The residents of Fort Myers continue to illustrate much resilience and fortitude as they restore their city.

Fun Fact: Fort Myers is known as the shelling mecca.

Restaurants:

To be honest many of my favorite hangout restaurants were located on Fort Myers Beach but hurricane Ian wiped nearly all of them out. It's hard to imagine the damage done by hurricane Ian but for those of us who grew up with our favorite eateries on the strip, it's a painful loss and now only memories. For example, Anthony's was one of my favorite places and I worked there during my college breaks. Wiped out. So for this portion of restaurants I'll be referring to a few restaurants in the Coconut Point area which technically is located in Estero. I particularly enjoy these restaurants and they are on the way to Fort Myers.

- **Ted's Montana Grill**: 8017 Plaza del Lago Dr, Estero, FL 33928 [Known for their bison hamburgers and chops.]

- **Divieto Ristorante**: 23161 Village Shops Way #101, Estero, FL 33928 [I had the salmon and loved it.]

- **Mama Anna Trattoria**: 23111 Fashion Dr, Estero, FL 33928 [Super cozy ambiance and the food was really delicious and the dishes were enormous.]

- **Ford's Garage**: 10801 Corkscrew Rd Suite 519, Estero, FL 33928 [An American menu and they use angus beef which I prefer. They have TV too so you can watch your favorite sport. Oh, and they are decorated with vintage Ford vehicles throughout.]

Hidden Gems:

Edison and Ford Winter Estates
2350 McGregor Blvd,
Fort Myers, FL 33901
Edisonfordwinterestates.org
Cost: $18-$30

The Edison and Ford Winter Estates stand as one of my all-time favorite destinations in Southwest Florida. Steeped in history and adorned with stunning botanical gardens, this remarkable site offers breathtaking views of the Caloosahatchee River. It's a perfect choice for a non-beach day excursion, where the blend of historical intrigue and natural beauty creates an experience that simply cannot be missed. Whether you're a history buff, a nature enthusiast, or just looking for a unique day out, the Edison and Ford Winter Estates are sure to leave a lasting impression.

I literally visit each year and make it a day trip. Pack my lunch and snacks and away I go. I enjoy going through Edison's museum and listening to the audio guide tours of each invention and envisioning what Edison was thinking at that moment. It's like walking back in time.

You may wonder why there is a botanical garden on the grounds and this is because Edison was a fabulous gardener and loved testing an array of plants and such. As soon as you enter the property, you are overtaken by the beauty of the plants, trees and flowers that Edison planted so many years ago.

Did you know that Henry Ford and Thomas Edison were good friends? Ford actually worked for the Detroit Edison Illuminating Company in the 1890's. When Ford came to visit Edison in Ft. Myers, he fell in love with the property and bought right next door to his friend. He gave Edison a Ford car every year too. You can see a few of Ford's cars parked in the garage on the property as well.

I could probably write a whole book on the Edison and Ford Winter Estates because I love it so much and have been visiting it for nearly 30 years. They offer events throughout the year but seriously if you're here at Christmas, you need to see how they deck out the place. Have I convinced you yet that you absolutely need to visit here?

Dim Jandy Ranch
13151 Pinto Ln,
Fort Myers, FL 33912
Dimjandy.com
Cost: $15/$30

You ready for this one? Dim Jandy Ranch is all about goats, specifically G.O.A.T (Greatest of All Time) Yoga. They offer 1.5 hours of yoga with their Nigerian dwarf goats and 15 min of goat snuggling. How precious is this? I told you I'm all about animals.

You will need to bring your own mats and book your reservation but they provide the cutest, sweetest goats ever. They have some other animals at the ranch too as well as an airbnb.

If you need some good, clean energy vibes, then you must visit G.O.A.T yoga.

The Shell Factory & Nature Park
2787 N Tamiami Trail
North Fort Myers, FL 33903
Shellfactory.com
Cost: $$

The Shell Factory has been around for 80 years and I can remember when my dad took my sister and me. Granted it's nothing like it was back then, but I have fond memories just the same. My favorite memory was 'pick a pearl' and I was so excited to find my very own freshwater pearl. It was equivalent to winning the lottery in my child's mind. They still have 'pick a pearl' and The Shell Factory is bigger and better with so many things to choose from.

- The Christmas House: the largest Christmas shop with over 1000 ornaments and it's Christmas all year long at this house. Super fun!
- The Fun Park: Tell me these activities don't look like fun to you.

1. Water Wars
2. Gem Mining
3. Zip line
4. Bummer boats
5. Paddle boats
6. Climbing wall
7. Carousal
8. Redneck shooting gallery
9. Climbing Pole

- The Nature Park: 4.5 acres of Florida animals rescued and so much more

1. Pet Farm
2. Gator Slough
3. Butterfly garden
4. Averie

Note: If you're a military vet, The Shell Factory & Nature Park offers discounts to you; it's their way of honoring the vets who served our country.

And yes, they do have a restaurant on the grounds so you can come and stay for the day without having to leave the property.

Escape Room Adventures
   12995 S Cleveland Ave., #217
   Fort Myers, FL 33907
   Escaperoomadventures.com
   Cost: $36/person

Have you ever experienced an escape room adventure? Do you know what it is? Well, allow me to enlighten you.

Escape room adventures offer a unique and engaging experience that makes them both fun and worth the investment of your time and money. Here are several reasons why:

- **Team Building and Social Interaction**: Escape rooms are inherently collaborative, requiring teamwork and communication. This makes them an excellent activity for friends, family, and even colleagues, as you work together to solve puzzles and achieve a common goal.

- **Mental Challenge**: These adventures provide a series of puzzles and riddles that challenge your problem-solving skills, logical reasoning, and sometimes, your knowledge. This mental stimulation can be incredibly satisfying, especially when you crack a particularly tough puzzle. (Now, if you came to Southwest Florida to enjoy our pristine beaches but you need a non-beach day because you're burned to a crisp, this is a perfect adventure. Your brain may be a bit baked too so the mental challenge of escape rooms may stretch you but don't despair, you will be able to escape and have fun doing it. Just my two cents.)

- **Immersive Experience**: Many escape rooms are themed and designed to immerse you in a different world. Whether you're solving a mystery in a pharaoh's tomb or trying to escape from a space station, the high-quality settings and storylines engage your imagination and provide an escape from everyday life.

- **Adrenaline Rush**: Working against the clock to solve puzzles and "escape" before time runs out adds an exciting, adrenaline-pumping element to the experience. This can be thrilling and make for a memorable adventure.

- **Sense of Achievement:** Successfully completing an escape room, especially under time pressure, offers a sense of accomplishment. It's rewarding to see your efforts lead to a tangible result, which is part of the appeal.

- **Variety and Replay Value**: With a wide range of themes and difficulty levels, escape rooms offer a variety of experiences. Even if you've completed one, there are always new and different challenges to explore, which adds to their replay value.

- **Learning Opportunity**: Escape rooms can be educational, often requiring knowledge in history, language, science, or mathematics. They can be a fun way to learn new things or apply existing knowledge in a practical context.

- **Creating Memories**: The shared experience of working through an escape room creates lasting memories with your family and friends. It's an activity that you're likely to discuss and reminisce about long after the day is over.

In summary, escape rooms combine entertainment, intellectual challenge, and social interaction, making them a worthwhile experience for a wide range of people. Whether you're looking for a fun night out with friends, a team-building activity with colleagues, or a unique family outing, escape rooms have something to offer.

Convinced yet?

The Escape Room Adventures has several different levels of difficulty for each game and you need not worry about the appropriateness of the games for children. They don't use foul language or adult themes in their games. Isn't that refreshing? They recommend children playing be at least 9 years old but younger ones can accompany you as well. Just be aware you may need to explain concepts to them. Regardless, it's a fun time for 9 -99 years old.

Go to their website and reserve your time slot. Oh and your group can be from 2 to 7 participants. Sound fun? Let's make some memories.

5

Sanibel & Captiva Islands

Sanibel and Captiva Islands, near Fort Myers by way of the causeway, are renowned for their picturesque scenery and tranquil ambiance. Sanibel, the larger of the two, is famous for its world-class shelling beaches and the Sanibel Lighthouse. The island maintains a laid-back, natural environment with an emphasis on conservation, as seen in places like the J.N. "Ding" Darling National Wildlife Refuge, which offers a habitat for a diverse range of wildlife.

Captiva Island, connected to Sanibel by a small bridge, is smaller and provides a more secluded and exclusive feel. Known for its beautiful sunsets, Captiva is dotted with charming cottages, luxurious resorts, and offers an array of dining options, often with stunning views of the Gulf of Mexico.

Both islands boast pristine, sandy beaches, clear waters, and a relaxed pace of life. They are ideal destinations for those seeking a peaceful retreat with opportunities for outdoor activities such as fishing, biking, bird watching, and kayaking.

The unique charm of Sanibel and Captiva lies in their blend of natural beauty and a serene, unspoiled atmosphere, making them jewels of Florida's Gulf Coast. I highly recommend bringing your bikes or renting bikes on either island to explore the charm of both islands. There are great bike paths all along both islands.

Fun Fact: Sanibel and Captiva were landing locations for pirates in the 1700's. Blackbeard and Gasparilla being the most notorious pirates to have landed and hid away on these two islands.

Restaurants:

With hurricane Ian, Sanibel and Captiva were hit really hard. Countless residents lost their homes. Again, some of my favorite food places are gone or in the process of being rebuilt. Keep this in mind that several restaurants are open but with limited time and space so some have put food trucks in their parking lots to accommodate you while they rebuild.

- **Bleu Rendez-Vous**: 751 Tarpon Bay Road, Sanibel, FL 33957 [Open Tuesday - Saturday 4p.- till close.]

- **Cielo**: 1244 Periwinkle Way, Sanibel, FL 33957 [Open Tuesday - Saturday for lunch 11:30a.-3:30p.; dinner 4:30p - 8p.]

- **Doc's Ford Sanibel**: 2500 Island Inn Road, Sanibel, FL 33957 [Open daily 11a. - 10p.]

- **Jerry's Cafe**: 1700 Periwinkle Way, Sanibel, FL 33957 (inside Jerry's Grocery store) [Open daily 7a. - 2p.]

- **The Mucky Duck**: 11546 Andy Rosse Lane, Captiva, FL 33924 [Open daily 11:30a - 9p.]

- **Old Captiva House:** 15951 Captiva Dr.,Captiva, FL 33924 [Open daily 7:30a - 11a; 4:30p - 9:30p.]

- **Captiva Island Pizza**: 11511 Andy Rosse Lane, Captiva, FL 33924 [Open daily 11a. - 7p.]

Hidden Gems:

The Bubble Room
15001 Captiva Dr.
Captiva, FL 33924

Bubbleroomrestaurant.com
Cost: $$

The Bubble Room, located on Captiva Island, is an iconic and whimsical dining establishment that has been enchanting visitors since its inception in the 1970s. I remember coming to The Bubble Room as a kid and being absolutely mesmerized by all the Christmas vintage bubble lights throughout the entire restaurant. It's famous for its eclectic and over-the-top decor, the restaurant features a multi-level dining area filled with vintage toys, Christmas lights, antique photos, and a collection of nostalgic memorabilia from the 1930s and 1940s. Each room in The Bubble Room has its own unique theme, creating an atmosphere that is both festive and surreal. The staff encourage you to walk around and discover all the decor while you wait for your meal.

Known not just for its vibrant ambiance, The Bubble Room also serves a variety of hearty American cuisine, with a focus on fresh seafood and mouth-watering desserts, particularly its famous cakes which have become a must-try for visitors. In fact, if any of my neighbors find out I'm going to The Bubble Room, I get a list of the different cake slices I'm going to bring back for them. Each slice of cake is about the size of your head and when you take your first bite, you will think you have died and gone to heaven. The staff, dressed in scout uniforms, add to the quirky charm of the place, providing friendly and entertaining service. I love quirky charm. Don't you?

A visit to The Bubble Room is more than just a meal; it's an experience that engages all the senses, offering a trip down memory lane in a joyously eccentric setting. This makes it not just a restaurant, but a true Captiva Island attraction in its own right.

Currently at this publishing, The Bubble Room is not completely open as they are recovering from hurricane Ian; however, the Boop, right next door is serving sandwiches and their famous cakes. Two of the three buildings are open so they are making amazing progress. I'm certain they will be fully functional in 2024.

I didn't put The Bubble Room under the restaurant section because it truly is a historic, eclectic landmark worth visiting and the best hidden gem on Captiva in my opinion. It's been around for over forty years and the collection of Christmas toys and vintage bubble lights are from the 1930's - 1940's. We all are looking forward to when it's completely restored and open to the public.

Sanibel Lighthouse
112 Periwinkle Way.
Sanibel, FL 33957
Cost: None

The Sanibel Island Lighthouse, an iconic landmark, stands proudly at the eastern tip of Sanibel Island, Florida. Constructed in 1884, this historic lighthouse has been a guiding beacon for mariners for over a century.

The lighthouse is a popular spot for both locals and tourists, offering breathtaking views and an ideal location for shelling, fishing, and bird watching. The surrounding area, including a charming fishing pier and nature trails, provides a serene environment for visitors to enjoy the natural beauty of the Gulf Coast.

Though the lighthouse itself is not open to the public for climbing, its presence adds a nostalgic and historical charm to the Sanibel landscape. The nearby Lighthouse Beach Park is a perfect place for a leisurely stroll, picnicking, and soaking in the tranquil seaside ambiance. The Sanibel Island Lighthouse is not just a beacon for ships; it's a beloved emblem of the island's heritage and a must-visit for anyone exploring the idyllic shores of Sanibel.

Even after hurricane Ian in 2022, the lighthouse is still standing albeit the keeper's building was destroyed and one of the legs of the lighthouse was damaged. We are very grateful that the lighthouse still stands.

J.N. Ding Darling National Wildlife Refuge
1 Wildlife Dr.
Sanibel, FL 33957
fws.gov
Cost: $10/vehicle

Established in 1976, the refuge was named after Jay Norwood "Ding" Darling, a pioneering conservationist and Pulitzer Prize-winning political cartoonist. Darling played a crucial role in the creation of the refuge, initially through his efforts to block the sale of environmentally valuable land and later by personally drawing the original boundaries of the sanctuary. Thus, why the refuge was named after him.

The Wildlife Drive, a popular attraction, offers a scenic route for biking, walking, or driving, providing opportunities to spot a diverse array of wildlife such as alligators, ospreys, and roseate spoonbills. Have you seen a roseate spoonbill? Unique and pink. You'll know when you spot one. I get so excited when I see them.

This refuge is not only a haven for wildlife but also a testament to "Ding" Darling's vision and commitment to preserving natural habitats for future generations, making it a meaningful and enriching destination for all who visit.

Make a day of discovering Sanibel and Captiva islands. I have a hunch that once you do, you'll come back frequently.

6

Marco Island

Marco Island offers a blend of captivating history and natural beauty. Marco Island, the largest of Florida's Ten Thousand Islands, is known for its stunning beaches, turquoise waters, and luxurious resorts, but its history is just as rich and intriguing.

Inhabited by the Calusa Indians for thousands of years, Marco Island boasts a significant historical heritage. The Calusa were known for their complex society and impressive shell mounds, some of which can still be seen today. The island's modern development began in the late 1800s, but it was the 1960s that marked a turning point when the Mackle Brothers, prominent developers, transformed it into a sought-after destination with modern amenities, while still preserving much of its natural charm.

Fun Fact: Captain Bill Collier opened a hotel in 1896 on the island and it still stands today; it's the Olde Marco Inn. Collier County of Naples is named after Captain Bill Collier. Okay, I shared two fun facts with no extra charge.

Restaurants:

I don't eat as often as I like on Marco Island but when I do you'll find me at these casual dining places. Clients have also enjoyed the food and service of each eatery as well.

- **The Crazy Flamingo**: 1035 N. Collier Blvd, Marco Island, FL 34145 [Open daily]

- **The Speak Easy Marco Island**: 1106 1/2 N. Collier Blvd., Unit 104, Marco Island, FL 34145 [Open daily]

- **2Shea's Salty Dog**: 599 S. Collier Blvd., Unit 105, Marco Island, FL 34145 [Open daily]

- **Dolphin Tiki Bar & Grill**: 1021 Anglers Cove, Marco Island, FL 34145 [Open daily]

Hidden Gems:

The Otter Mound Preserve
1831 Addison Court

Marco Island, FL 33145
colliercountyfl.gov
Cost: None

Otter Mound Preserve on Marco Island, Florida, gets its name from the Calusa Indian shell mound dating back over a thousand years ago. This serene 2.5-acre preserve is nestled in the midst of a residential area, offering a peaceful escape into nature. The dense canopy, dominated by gumbo limbo trees, strangler figs, and slash pines, creates a cool, shaded trail, a stark contrast to the surrounding urban landscape.

The shell mounds were built from the discarded shells of

oysters, clams, and other shellfish, and served as elevated sites for habitation, ceremonial, and burial purposes. As you meander through the preserve's trails, you're literally walking atop centuries of history. Interpretive signage along the way provides insights into the lives of the Calusa Indians and the later settlers who farmed the land in the early 20th century.

I love when history combines with nature.

Note: The trail is not wheelchair accessible. There are no restroom facilities on site.

Goodlands
1831 Addison Court
Marco Island, FL 33145
colliercountyfl.gov
Cost: $$

Goodland, Florida, is this quirky little fishing village that feels like a step back in time, tucked away in a corner of Marco Island.

It's got a super laid-back, old Florida vibe that's a real breath of fresh air. The history of Goodland goes way back to the late 1800s when it was all about fishing and living off the land (or, well, the sea!). It's named 'Goodland' for a reason - the rich, fertile soil was perfect for growing fruit and vegetables. The place was kind of isolated until the 1930s, when a road finally linked it to the rest of Marco Island. Even today, with just a few hundred residents, Goodland feels like a close-knit community where everybody knows everybody.

You've gotta check out Stan's Idle Hour – it's practically an institution. On Sundays, they have this awesome outdoor party with live music that turns the whole place into a big, fun bash. Seafood lovers, rejoice! The local restaurants serve up some of the freshest catches around. Oh, and if you're into fishing, you're in for a treat. You can hop on a charter and try your luck catching snook, redfish, or tarpon. And for a bit of culture, swing by the Goodland Arts Alliance during one of their art festivals. It's like this cool mix of history, laid-back island life, and a little bit of partying – all in one neat, colorful package!

I stumbled on Goodland, Florida about six years ago on my way to Marco Island to meet with a client. I found Stan's and fell in love. The live music and yummy food keeps me coming back. There are a few airbnbs in Goodland too in case you want to spend the night and go fishing early the next morning.

7

Conclusion

Alright, let's wrap this up! We've had quite the adventure exploring Southwest Florida, haven't we? From the off the beaten path of Naples and its treasures, to the laid-back charm of Bonita Springs, each city we've visited has its own unique flavor. Fort Myers blew us away with its amazing trails, escape rooms and historical treasures - seriously, a must-see for any history buffs out there.

Then there was Sanibel, with its world-famous bike trails and the lighthouse that still stands and the stunning J.N. "Ding" Darling National Wildlife Refuge. Oh, and we can't forget Captiva, a little slice of paradise where the sunsets are just unreal and the cakes from The Bubble Room are divine. Marco Island treated us to the Otter Mound Preserve and some rich history, giving us that perfect mix of relaxation and exploration.

And Goodland? What a hidden gem! It's like stepping into another world where the pace slows down, and you can just enjoy the simple things in life. Each of these places, from Naples to Goodland, brings something special to the table, making Southwest Florida this incredibly diverse and endlessly fascinating region. Whether you're a beach bum, a nature enthusiast, a history geek, or in it for the hidden gems, Southwest Florida has got you covered. Safe travels, and don't forget to come back and explore some more – there's always something new to discover here!

If you enjoyed this pocket travel guide and found it useful, kindly leave a favorable review on Amazon.

8

Journal

Jot down your favorite memories from each hidden gem. You'll be glad you did.

Date: _____ Location:_____

What I loved about this hidden gem:
_____
_____

Date: _____ Location:_____

What I loved about this hidden gem:
_____
_____

Date: _____ Location:_____

What I loved about this hidden gem:
_____

Date: _____ Location:_____

What I loved about this hidden gem:

_____
_____

Date: _____ Location:_____

What I loved about this hidden gem:

_____
_____

Date: _____ Location:_____

What I loved about this hidden gem:

_____
_____

Date: _____ Location:_____

What I loved about this hidden gem:

_____
_____

Date: _____ Location:_____

What I loved about this hidden gem:

_____
_____

JOURNAL

Date: _____ Location: _____

What I loved about this hidden gem:

_____
_____

Date: _____ Location: _____

What I loved about this hidden gem:

_____
_____

Date: _____ Location: _____

What I loved about this hidden gem:

_____
_____

Date: _____ Location: _____

What I loved about this hidden gem:

_____
_____

9

Resources

Marco Island Beach Getaway. (n.d.). *Marco Island Beach Getaway.* https://marcoislandbeachgetaway.com/

Marco Island Beach Getaway. (2020, March 30). *A brief history of Marco Island, Florida - Marco Island Beach Getaway.* https://marcoislandbeachgetaway.com/marco-island-history/

Madmin, & Madmin. (2023, April 8). *Spend the day at Marco Island's Otter Mound Preserve.* Clausen Properties Inc. https://escapetomarco.com/spend-the-day-at-marco-islands-otter-mound-preserve/

https://colliercountryfl.gov/government/public-services/divisions/conservation-collier/preserve-information/otter-mound

https://thescancapguide.com/restaurants/which-restaurants-are-open-on-sanibel-after-hurricane-2023/

RESOURCES

Sanibel Lighthouse - Point Ybel Light. Sanibel, Florida, USA. (2020, March 3). VistaCreate. https://create.vista.com/photos/sanibel-island/

Adventures, E. R. (n.d.). *Escape room adventures.* Escape Room Adventures. https://escaperoomadventures.com/

Fort Myers Museums, attractions, things to do | Edison Ford Winter Estates. (2022, July 7). Edison and Ford Winter Estates. https://www.edisonfordwinterestates.org/

https://www.dimjandyranch.com

The Shell Factory. (n.d.). https://www.shellfactory.com/

Shy Wolf Sanctuary. (2024, January 6). *- Shy Wolf Sanctuary.* https://www.shywolfsanctuary.org/

Naples Florida Paved Nature Trail | Gordon River Greenway. (2022, May 12). Gordon River Greenway. https://gordonrivergreenway.org/

Holocaust Museum & Education Center. (2024, January 4). *Home | Holocaust Museum & Education Center.* https://hmcec.org/

CREW Land & Water Trust. (2022, December 14). *Trail Use Guidelines » CREW Land & Water Trust.* https://crewtrust.org/home/trail-guidelines/

Printed in Great Britain
by Amazon